More praise for *Nike Adjusting Her Sandal*

"Three thousand ancestors ask how I straddle / the sea, a foot on Anastasia Vassos writes. One answer is this lovely book, which begins and ends in Greece, the home of both her ancestors and the mythological and literary figures she references throughout. Woven through the geographical fabric is a loose chronological thread connecting a midwestern childhood, a lasting love relationship, and the aging of parents. "Let me be a book before it's written," Vassos writes. Here is the book, written, with its vivid imagery, its attention to sound and form, its "words lined up . . . behind the heart."
— **Martha Collins**

Listen to how Anastasia Vassos recasts Cavafy in the precisely-measured, spare intensities of her own desire-haunted voice: "I look for our bench.... / I think it was this one. / I remember how we sat here / in the beginning / trying to resist each other. / How we tried to end it / and couldn't." And here are her eloquent lines of traditional lament: "This bitter-ash season of your death, / when we lit yellow candles that burned long and bright / little chevrons of pain pointing to heaven, / the air close, the heart closed."

Between the demands of the erotic and the dearness of the familial, between Eros and Agape, the triumph of *Nike Adjusting Her Sandal* is in the poise of the poems, as ready for lyric flight as they are prepared for our earth-bound human condition.
— **George Kalogeris**, author of *Guide to Greece*

Nike Adjusting Her Sandal

ANASTASIA VASSOS

Nixes Mate Books
Allston, Massachusetts

Book design by d'Entremont
Cover photograph by Gary Koeppel

ISBN 978-1-949279-32-0

Nixes Mate Books
POBox 1179
Allston, MA 02134
nixesmate.pub

In Memory of Denny Donaldson

Seize the Day

Contents

Nike Adjusting Her Sandal

I

Thessaloniki, 4 AM

Here they dance with arms raised above their heads
the middle of the body suspended like a question.

They bend their knees as their feet
describe the arc of some forgotten journey.

I've been up all night drinking ouzo, my plane
leaves in an hour, the rebetika pulses

in my veins. I have an exquisite headache. I'm in love
with this city of dusty streets and ancient churches.

For now, it is I on this empty road, the car radio
my only cohort. Metallic strains of bouzouki seep

through the air like the thick smoke of a Gauloise.
Even the sardine fishermen sleep.

The heat has begun to settle, a blanket.
When the sun comes up, I'll be gone.

Three thousand ancestors ask how I straddle
the sea, a foot on either shore.

I peer through the windshield at Orion's belt
in search of home. The three sisters

are the stars that shine in the middle.
I race through the dark, speaking in tongues.

On Thira

On this white island ringed in blue and dust
we climb ghost steps leading up,
out of the cauldron.

You and I are Greeks, today,
pretending we're on the surface
of the moon.

A widow dressed in black
guards the church.

Here at the edge of the Aegean
she tells us
there's more wine than water,
more churches than houses
more donkeys than people.

Feed me a country that curves
rogue waves round its edge,
then returns them.
I thirst. I hunger.

Baffled crater!
Caldera. Caldaria.
Language laces my Greek tongue
with the lips of a Spaniard.

We're at the hem
of the volcano.
I lift my dress,
the breeze on my legs.

Caldera

We sit on the rim of Crater Lake
on a day so clear that the birds keen
silently, and the water sweeps
so blue, so sharply blue it slices our sight
and candles bob the surface.
You hold a bright red tomato,
your hand surrounds
it like a plush old chair. You draw
your knife across the inflated middle
with the molten grace of a cellist pulling
his bow across the crescent
body of a hollow spruce.

It's like sitting on top of the world,
isn't it – and we command it.
If we were trees, we would bend
to this old wind.

Ars Poetica

Many angels to wish
whole again:
white wings fall
from a pin,
words escape
the runway
of the tongue,
desire seeps
from the body
in a stream.

I ponder the dark illiteracies that cannot be undone:
a pomegranate, an apple.

Let me be a book before it's written.
Words lined up in proper order behind the heart.
Pomegranate seeds that glow like garnets
cleaving to white pith inside red, burly skin.

The Others

Mother's right hand
spins the wheel
of her black
and silver Singer.
Her left guides fabric
underneath the presser foot,
the needle hooks
thread from down
below the bobbin.
She manages the straightest seams.
I sit on the attic floor
and watch. My legs make
the letter *V, as in Victory,*
V for Vassos.
Before I run, I will grow
up in this house.

I stand beside
the other girls, later.

The other girls
 – in their oxfords
and bobby sox –
slouch in those collared
shirts poking out
of their lop-sided sweaters.
I wear white gloves,
stare down the camera,
my little straw purse
dangles from my wrist.
Patent leather shoes,
crisp yellow dress.

Point of Origin

Grapevines tangle the maple tree.
Long-haired Moirai ravel destiny.
Sunlight of August pitches and lingers.
I remember: string tied to my finger,

holding then losing a red balloon,
lilies of the valley, hollow moons.
I've changed my clothes three times today,
the path unstitched geography.

Mother pedals her Singer machine
to make my clothes, I hear her singing.
Whirr of work, she won't look back:
pins that snare, thread that snaps

through delicate fabric. Scissors that scare.
My Sisters – *the sparing ones* – are here.

Eye of the Needle

On the night Sirhan Sirhan shot Bobby Kennedy in the kitchen of the Ambassador Hotel in California, my mother sat in our red TV room, head bent next to the lamp, and placed a thimble on her finger. She pulled a needle from the plump, scarlet pincushion, held it up to the light, and surrendered white thread to the eye. She held the hem of my prom dress between her left thumb and forefinger. The pocked cap of the thimble thrust the needle and claimed the fabric. *Put it on, now. Let's see how it looks.* I turned, slowly, while she made sure the hem was straight.

a forgotten needle
pricks my ankle
draws a drop of blood

Prodigal Daughter

He stood,
poured his tea
from one cup
to another to cool,
so he could drink it
before he walked
to the corner
of the street to catch a bus
that took him to the train,
to walk another block
to catch another bus
and then walk to his store,
so that my sister and I
could go to college.

I paid my father back
by telling him
I didn't believe in God.

That was the summer
I memorized Yeats
as I rode the train
to work in town.
I stared at the outlines of trees
against the sky's coat.

He called me *Princess*.

He faltered into the chair
next to the phone
on the wall,
he said *that's a sin, you know* –
and I, in my know-it-all-ness,
with my *college education*,
was indifferent
until my mother
told me he cried.
I had been thinking
about Petrarchan sonnets
and that I had run out of cigarettes.

How I Did It

How the moon kicked over the bucket.
How I carried the pail on my shoulders.
How nightfall burnished the knife.
How light travelled in the dark
    like a running river.
How I caught the river and sluiced
    her secret.
How I cut my hand.

How I entered screaming.
How I told the story in reverse.
How I wrote in cursive
    with my opposing hand.
How the boat stayed hollow.
How the river turned in on itself.
How I almost drowned.
How the dog barked.
How the night swallowed.
How I tasted metal.
How it stuck in my throat.

Tinos, August 2012

The island holds dust like a bowl,
but not for long. When the wind cracks,
the sand snakes. The priest's shutters
are open. The rooster blusters
the morning sun.

In the center of the powdery town
a modern-day Sisyphus ascends
to the Virgin Mary's church on hands
and knees – the bone he has to pick
with God between his teeth.
Dust in his lungs, his coarse face
is flooded blood-hot, a scrim of heat
rises off his back like a mirage.

We walk the sandy roads hand
in hand and observe this sacred contour.
We stop for bread, tomatoes, cheese.
A bottle of water. We bow our heads
having never been hungry.

Alexandria

Cavafy, you walked here, the vision
of your last lover up ahead, out of reach.
Ancestor, you wandered alone,
the hot consoling daydreams burning.

If memory distilled an odor, this would be it,
the sweet burr in the nostrils, streets furred
with incense, the censor swinging
through the streets' naked corridors.

Once, a library burned here.
Once, there was a lighthouse here.

Where the Nile brims into the Mediterranean,
and the waves remember their Greek,
Hedone rides like a tide, returning.

Walking Home from the Poetry Salon

Friday night. Midsummer.
The city's palm faces up in surrender.

The air clings, the night prowls.
Veil of cologne. Hormones trail the air.

No time to sleep.
Pedestrians shove time in their pockets.

Slick with sweat of not having, the streets slip.
Desire leaks into air like cigarette smoke.

I smoulder. Put a match to my skin.
It catches like paper.

In Prague

That night the Charles Bridge boiled –
it was choked with people
crossing over the Vitava River.
Somnambulists were out.

Down the alley in the Old Town
the beggar sat alone
dressed in black, toe to head
but for the boiled egg whites
of his eyes and the pink
of his lips glowing
against his other nothingness.
You dared me to say something
though he was mute.
I wore the tie-dyed
shirt you like: the color
of clouds at midnight.

Later, in our room overlooking
the black stone clock tower
the moon shifted under my skin.

Cleft

Meaning parting of the thighs
meaning, o love, the holy way
meaning sculpted mark, glyph
meaning the way we find
into one another's angles,
the hieroglyph
of my head on your shoulder
as you thin
your film of sweat
my center cleaves a path,
my center cleaves to you.

Ekinlik Island

A baby girl born in a hut, a dot
in the middle of the sea,
lifted off the bed,
staring into black waters –
Sea of *Marmara*, Sea of Marble.

The full moon scrapes the cold surface –
the prow of the ship chops
the way a knife chops onions.

A woman stands in her kitchen,
let's say it's I who turns the pages
of a recipe book. The cutting
board's scratches rough to touch.
I have time to endure.

I am curious, Mother,
about a vessel crossing the ocean,
fingers trailing, your cries
falling across the waves.

Portrait of Mother on the Greek Peninsula

The yellow ladder leaned against the white
house, gleaming. The baby swallows tilted and swerved
in cursive against the bluest sky. That was the summer
you had the best idea, the summer you laid
the hose out in the sun so we'd have hot water.

On the simmering beach, you sat with your hat
on your head in the doubtful shade
of the rusty umbrella, you sat next to your sister
on the crisp edge of the sea, watching the sea
watching my sister and me swim in the bluest sea.

You sat on the shimmering beach, I swam in the bluest
sea with my sister. The summer you had the best
idea. We picked kumquats from trees that lined the garden
like old time Greek soldiers in layered skirts, ate kumquats
while the baby swallows curled their tongues around songs.

The sun was so hot we could have melted butter on stones
at sunrise, we laid out the garden hose for water
hot enough to wash off the salt and sand from the simmering
beach. The best idea. Your hat on your head, you washed
my shirt till it was whiter than white in the hottest sun

ironed my shirt to its crispest edge, as white as the house
that held the yellowest ladder that leaned
against it, gleaming, you were the best that summer.
I remember that summer as if it were just now
like the answer to a question leaning in a doorway.

II

Nike Adjusting Her Sandal

after the sculpture "Nike Adjusting Her Sandal" at Temple of Athena Nike, Acropolis

It was Plato
who did not say,
but surely reflected: shadows
conscript the sun
to show true Form.

You stop, breathless.
Water folds down the front
of your body, the dim
fabric of a chiton.
You balance on one leg.

Ars Poetica

Too close to the sun.
What clusters in the wax?
What feathers in the mouth?

What remains of your heart:
a play, a form, sound-sense: incantation.
Words cluster: legacy feathers
its way down a ladder
to reach you.

Being Middle Aged Back Then

I could have forgotten
but didn't.
I've been thinking
about him all day
and now the afternoon
gives way
and slowly folds
into the envelope of twilight –
I'll sink my eyes
on him at night.

I walk along
the Charles River Esplanade
across the pink stucco
Fiedler Bridge.
The sun behind me
pushes my shadow
down Charles Street
across the cobblestones

the sun's rays
bounce like hot oil
off the State House dome.
Past the brass ducklings'
worn sheen
in the Public Garden.

I look for our bench.
I believe in
keeping promises.
Maybe my ancestors
worshipped adulterous gods.
No matter who said what
I long for no one
but him.

I think it was this one.
I remember how we sat here
in the beginning
trying to resist each other.
How we tried to end it
and couldn't.

To the Flowering Dogwood We Planted Next to the House

After the weeks of jolting
our decision after hours
of having maybe
preferred the Coral Bark
or the Japanese Maple,
we brought you home in a hurry.
To be honest, we were afraid
for you, for the sun that would beat
down, a summer drum
on your head in the southwest
corner of the yard.
But you were the one I wanted
all along, your four-petalled
pink flowers bravely holding
the air, dimpled palms
to keep our courage up in spring
when the world smells like
startled lemons.

After the light-and-death discussions
we brought you home to us
knowing you'd survive
in the light that might
scrutinize you, there,
next to the house.
Now, when I am away from you
my heart folds – cinched –
until I see you again.
You stand, a tall thin sister
in the corner of the yard
a breathing being like me
that I can talk to when
the birds rain enough songs down
to fill a barrel, while I stroke
your new leaves
that hang folded and wet
like a calf being born.

Apollo Rising

My last memory of the old stairs out back is slipping on the top step in the rain, landing on my coccyx. *Sure thing, baby* you winked when I asked you to build a deck to replace the trivial platform and rickety stairs to the house. You flew in, my Apollo, skidding to a stop with two forty-pound bags of cement, and a cement mixer to churn the yearnings of our burning hearts. Your muscles bulged like the sound of bugles, heralds of loudest light. You wore a skin-tight t-shirt. You filled the footings and stayed the night. We slept with windows open.

Now the days slip backwards, grow short. Here we sit, the city laid out before us. The old chairs comfort us. The wind picks up from the northeast, the clouds skid across. Through breaks in the billows the sun beats its rhythm into my skin. I shade my eyes with my hand to regard you. Ask myself where did twenty five years go, in what worn valise did they carry our youth and vigor, so carelessly thrown into the carriage of our wanting.

Nike Adjusting Her Sandal

after the sculpture "Nike Adjusting Her Sandal" at Temple of Athena Nike, Acropolis

How light creates folds across her dress
a water shimmer, a shiver trick
of the eye, unadorned, exquisite.

Time-wrinkles, ages passing
a narrow road of shade
amid the gladness of riot light.

She steps across one poem at a time
her feet wet with words
the subtle harmony of some unknown thing.

Bittersweet

As if the matriarch who died last year
could hear her, Barbara says *sorry, Andree*
as we hack away at the Oriental Bittersweet.
It's clung to the porch's iron railing
for fifty years. Its little orange capsules hold
red seeds that will never take hold
because of our necessary task.

We make our saddest effort cleaning up
the garden for winter. Yesterday, we pitch-forked
the pile of wood chips at the top of the hill,
moved them down the path to the hollow,
barrow by barrow, almost as far as the bridge.
Behind our backs, the red maple in the center
of the yard had dropped her yellow skirt.

The bittersweet won't grow back –
we've made sure of that – it's invasive,
non-native, and we've hacked it down
to its stubby root. But the iris that we split,

rhizomes bleached in a ten
percent solution, will take hold
once spring comes, and push their spathes
toward the sun, standards blazing, beards
almost psychedelic in their insistence.

Such is the stubbornness of nature.
She plays dead, then comes back to life
like Lazarus, who could not stay
underground for more than four days
before he was revived.

Weight of Air

Barometric pressure slices
layers of my skin.

The horizon's flat belly scrapes the sky.
A table waits to be set.

Clouds strew themselves to windshields.
Empty plates.

The Midwest hungers.
Knives and forks dissect the air.

Different Death

for Anne Sexton

Let me lead you
to a different death.
Let me hold you, too
tight in the grip
of a sorry mouth.
The arguments of light
in the city windows
blind our eyes
and the setting sun
incinerates our backs.
The voices of furious robins
choke in the innocent throat.
Once you were the child
on the swing, the sun
rushing down like a flood
of butter on skinny
legs pumping.

You would have trespassed
your eighty-eighth
year this year.
Let me try to imagine
the crooked mouth
blinking away cigarette smoke
from eyes the color
of noon, the trail of breath
the errant flame.
A thousand poems
consuming you
like a deep and narrow river
or an unmade bed.

On Eleuthera

You point out
the North Star
at the tip of Ursa Minor.
The Bear is barely visible.
Your voice points
past my shoulder –
there's the Little Dipper
and Stella Polaris
dancing at the top
of the handle.
And I look up
and back at your face.

The sky is so black,
there is a kind
of synesthesia afoot –
touching stars
before hearing them –
and the seeing!

That was the summer
after your chemo,
when you slept
most days,
your spontaneous *epistaxis*
dripping blood
out of nowhere
it seemed, you holding
our beach towels up
to your nose,
stanching the mess
and there we were,
on Eleuthera's
Atlantic side –
wild, slate, blue.

That was the summer
you convinced me
that night joins opposites,
fear and love, nothing
and morning – that ebony night,
those fulgid stars.

Aurora Borealis

My ear's snail
— shaped cochlea picks up
hush and swing.
The sky rinses her hair
in magenta.
Water falling.

Sweet trail of light
the snail leaves behind.
Opalescent murmur.

Low vibration of a train,
before it reaches the station.
A remnant remembered
arcs toward the beloved.

A pulse,
a neural quiver
between two synapses.
The sun's charged particles.

The souls of ancestors
whisper prayers
to the living.

The Night Train

She appeared
then turned in the doorway

like a jewel striking the sun
before she was gone.

That night on the late train
from Thessaloniki to Athens

I twisted and turned
like wild, waist-length hair

braided and shaped
into an ancient grey knot.

Self Portrait As Jane Kenyon

It's the end of May.
The sun rises late here
in the Midwest, as I did
this morning. Mother still sleeps.
I will wake her soon.

Caring for her these days
is like trying to carry water in my palm
over a long distance. When she is gone
I'll wish for them back.

The sky started out blue
but the islands that were clouds
now cling to one another
and portend rain. Nature
upturns herself.

So be it. The ground is as dry
and cracked as an old woman's skin.
Three birds sing, a tree waves.
Cool wind from the west.

Driving to Lake Erie on Mother's 97th Birthday

The late October light has weakened
my resolve for heroism.

Mother and I drive east, the lake to our left,
its furthest coast another country.

To our right, maple leaves' cinders
singe the sidewalk's gray vestiges, leave scars.

A lonely teenager rakes the clamorous
debris, her red hair drowns her shoulders.

Over our heads, the clouds hold
their convocation. And the sparrows

have gathered their tribe:
now a hundred arrows released

and turned by the wind.
Mother curves her head:

she hears but does not see.
If I didn't know better I'd say

when it's time to die, try to face north.
The light remains constant there.

Sisterland

I've been waiting for the sun
to rise, your collarbone a horizon
and the world starts fresh.

Strange gauze of your stare
as you wipe away dreaming.
And I, sitting on the side of the bed

in the curve your body makes,
lambent light elbowing its way in –
I woke you too early, sleep a little longer.

III

The Day Jack Gilbert Kissed Me

On father's birthday I took flowers.
The dirt from his grave stuck

to the underside of my fingernails.
I grew up on this dirt

that stretches and does not end.
The epitaph burnished by the blade

of sun setting on the grave.
The robin's red breast bigger

than a Mack truck. When I turn
my back the robin turns

into my poem.

Truly, Really

This almost-October afternoon of Indian summer
is so filled with light, the sun so yellow
the air, like butter, melts in my mouth,
bakes apples on the tongue.

This bitter-ash season of your death,
when we lit yellow candles that burned long and bright,
little chevrons of pain pointing to heaven,
the air close, the heart closed.

Rosy morning opened her robe in the rain, and shivered.
Now, the day is so filled with sun, so filled with heat,
I could weep. I was eight when you brought us

fresh figs, your pleasure spilling like warm syrup,
the afternoon ablaze like this one. *Eat*, you said,
they ripened in the sun, you won't believe the taste.

Sappho

after the painting "Sappho" by August Mengin

Your face is a tablecloth waiting to be set.
Your breasts, spoons waiting to be emptied.
Your hair weeps: a cataract.

The waves of the Aegean are arms
with foam tattoos rowing
against the moon's urgent gravity.

You pull us into the tenebrous abyss
where rocks wear skirts. You said

remember whom you leave shackled by love
and then plunged your eyes
like weighted curtains left in the rain.

Oneiric Means Dreamlike

An armful of rain is carried
across the sky on a young woman's
head. She trips and spills
her charge into the basket

of our dream. The stream of drops
becomes a fog of clouded sound –
the echo of a Buddhist *rin gong* –
nothing more
                          than rain holding its breath.
Sometimes we tire of the brain's
habits and long for the pill of light
on the tongue of night.

This morning she stepped across the roof
of our silences and we sat up, blinking.

This Body, Your Body

What if this body your body be broken
and numbers mean naming along a great distance –
your body part one, doctor beside
Anastasia part two, cupping a bowl.

This body, this horse you ride to the ocean
the hoofbeats, the gallons, the shelf on the beach.
You reach a dimension, the days lie like showers
of paper the wind could dispense with a blow.

But time brutes so slowly on sand made of water
our feet sink like anchors, we're anchored to nothing
nothing by reason, the seasons outnumbered
bewitched by destruction, by innocent bliss.

My love, keep your body beside me forever –
the gallop, the naming will bring us to this.

At Symphony Hall

Lights dim whispers
to cloudfalling quiet.
Sound pushes to its origin.

Yo-Yo Ma pulls
his threaded needle
through a gallon cello.

A cantilena ravels –
what Pythagoras heard
when the planets chanted.

Sappho In Translation

I shall kiss
becomes
I shall love
according to the translator
who thinks she knows
better than Sappho.

I prefer the bitter
weapon of kissing –
the mouth the charged
organ of love's longing.

And speaking
of hunger
how does the sun
manage to slice
the air
to create shadow?

I Will Forgive

September is the best month for dying.
Sun's blade sharpens its point. Birds stop
declaring they want to stay. The smell of rain
pervades. Leaves from old-growth trees leave
permanent tattoos on the pavement.
Were I to shoulder my grief into the folds
of my favorite sweater, you would tell me
to remember how much you loved me. You insisted.
We were finely stitched, edged in bone and blood.
Now my hindsight unravels its tangled net.
A keen knife slices night from day. I remember,
as you could not, your words before you left us
for those porous borders. Remember?
How you made us learn prayers in ancient Greek?
Syllable by syllable. We clenched our teeth to God.
We gave him a name. Say *maker*. Say *middle distance*.
Cold shudder in my ear. Sense could not be made.
Autumn unleafing, then, the stinging time of year.
If you get another chance, please name me Moira.
For *bitter*. For *fate*.

Sisterland

Remind me to tell you how the sun
bounces shadows when we're apart.

The thin reed of your frailty
falls from brown paper bags turned

upside down. Try on my coat.
Sleeves a little long, but it fits and it's warm.

Listen: you remember all the words
to Greek hymns we learned

as children. I mouth the songs
in church a half second behind you.

This is how we wander,
hand inside hand since Mother died.

Where are the clouds. How does one think
with no sky overhead.

the modern poet tries to read Sappho in ancient Greek

        ] yes

] on a soft bed

] one

        cycladic beckon [   ] found

] not found

] yearns

her virginity

O for Adonis

] lyre

] necessary limb [

] *bride with beautiful feet*

] pearls
unstrung

] Orpheus ungrounded [   ] decoded

] imaginal [   ] smears
hands dip [   ] yes

] language
                ] lingual
                        ] languor
                                ] linger

] lost [   ] soft

  ] ah ah Sappho

stand to face me beloved and open out [

the grace of your eyes

and so [   ] sensate dream

] and these fingertips

and on these eyes[   ] yes

    black sleep of night

words linger now [   ] yes
      tongue lips bloom on ear

may you sleep on the breast of your delicate friend

Chariot

I need my sunglasses
and blame my headache

on the long drive
from Cleveland to Boston.

When I left her hospice bed,
the roses on her dresser shimmered.

In the Midwest time zone,
they lose light last.

Self Portrait As Lot's Wife

Nature has abandoned me.
This morning when I awoke
the birds were still. The willow
in the garden had flung her branches
along the ground like the hair
of a woman strangled. The rain
slipped down like the fingers
of a careless, sleeping god, unfurled.

I stand at the edge of my life.
I wrap my coat about me – my pearls
become tangled in my sleeve.
I brush my hair from my eyes.
I stand sentry to dreams not remembered.
I am a pedestal – I am a book
about to be written. I am a soothsayer.
Tonight will be the night of broken lives.

And what will be my crime?
To turn my head to the left, my hair

flung about the opposite shoulder
like a spray of thunder, rain
or gravel, words or pearls taunted
by the gods of unknown sin? I lean
my question in the doorway. I crack
old cups and toss them into the fire.
I walk away.

Eight Years After

I'm cutting olives for my lunch. It's a rainy afternoon. I stand at the kitchen counter slicing the fleshy tissue away from the pit of each one. Nothing satisfies me like olives when I'm hungry. The way the salt of them fills my still inside and brings on more appetite. The skin resists the pinch of my knife, but once pierced, the olive offers its brown speckled flesh to my hand.

You are so real at this moment, standing over my shoulder. I recall our penultimate moment, though I didn't know it at the time. The day I left Thessaloniki for Santorini, you handed me a plastic bucket of olives to fortify me on the trip. Later, I spent afternoons on the island sitting on a metal chair on the edge of the caldera, staring out at the volcano, drinking beer and eating those olives, one by one.

> last night's thunder –
> somewhere
> a man has died

My Childhood Friend Is Dying

We didn't know then you could die of cancer.
We ran to the corner and back, before cancer.

Summer hair falls like steel plumbed lines
impelled to gravity. Raining cancer.

Mutation devours the flowers we picked outside.
The insidious snake slithers through cancer.

Ride a bike across a bridge on fire.
Double-cross, furious smear of cancer.

She houses illusion's guest, but the sovereign
of maladies cooks unseen. His name is Cancer.

The best she can brawl on the end of this limb.
She fights like a girl, but she'll fall into cancer.

This grave-dug life holds mercy obscured
and dim within its layers. Fuck cancer.

My name, Anastasia, means *life after death*.
World without Lynn: still life with cancer.

Sappho Contemplates Suicide at Lefkada

Here, on the torn cliff.
Look. A boat sails below.

Smell of hyacinth, rush of air.
Even wind envies me, my ruthlessness.

Cup of wine spills over rock. A prayer.
Beloved's name forms the cave of my mouth.

Waves lay the tunic's hem at my feet.
In the distance: the Sirens.

End of Life Directive

Have you written a will.
Who is your next of kin. Are you of right mind.
If you are incapacitated, then what. Can you articulate
your wishes. Should we resuscitate. Will you hear singing.
How many voices on the head of a pin.
How loud is too loud.

Are you smitten. Where is the muscle
in the main. Are you tattooed. Cursive or typed.
Cash or credit. Do you want the Lord to take you. Do you
know the Lord. How will we meet in the sweet after-after.
Do you know how to fly. Are you afraid to die.
Do you hear buzzing.

Do you believe in reincarnation.
Will you leave your ring under my pillow. Will you come back
as a crow. Will you come back in hijab. How long have you been
a Christian. Who will you see in heaven. Do Buddhists believe
in breath after death.

Who will bury you. Paper or plastic.
How will you burn. How hot. How should white linen drape
the body. How will ashes scatter if wind blows from the East.
Will you face North. Will you feed a hemlock. What is the color
of the wine-dark sea.

Diaspora

The island of Tinos
is home to West Wind, I learned, right after
Mantho's friend rented me the car
and told me to hold tight to the handle
when I opened the door so it wouldn't
rip off or I'd have to buy a new one.
The wind throws dust
onto every possible surface.
I park in the driveway and hold tight
to the handle.

*

I'm at the age where I trust
night to shift into day. Here in the pulse
of morning I measure my heartbeats
with words. Boston is a wet gray bowl,
far from the olive tree on grandmother's
land. She made a deal in exchange
for two apartments and a marble foyer.
A stump stands in what's left of the yard.

*

I am home, and far from it.
Zephyrus rushes rain into my window
and slices the silence.
Water pours into the ground.

*

In Thessaloniki, I visit the cemetery
with my aunt to see the grave
of her mother, my grandmother.
We pass naked excavations that once
honored sacred remains. What's left,
delved among bones of the dead, are three-
cornered heads of coffins, exposed in the dirt.
There's no land, my aunt explains.
After a while, we just need to make room.
She's dead now too.

*

The accents and letters of my Greek ancestors
gutter in my mouth. *Parakalo-efharisto.*
Beginning-end. Alpha-omega.

There's no end to the combinations
I could make. I translate Greek to English,
English to Greek. Every word made up of two.
Iconoclast. Nostalgia. Dyslexic.

*

To remind myself where I'm headed,
I throw ashes at the ancestors.

Notes

Caldera is for Roger Auerbach.

Tinos, August 2012 is dedicated to Patrice Martin.

To the Flowering Dogwood We Planted Next to the House is for Marge Piercy.

Bittersweet is for Barbara Trainer.

On Eleuthera is for David Hartranft.

The ninth line in *Sappho* is a fragment from a translation by Mary Barnard.

The third line in *Sappho in Translation* is taken from Sappho's fragment 88A, from Anne Carson's translation "If Not, Winter" (First Vintage Books Edition, Random House, 2003).

the modern poet tries to read Sappho in ancient Greek includes italicized phrases from the following fragments of Sappho, translated by Anne Carson: 168, 103b, 138, 151, 126.

My Childhood Friend Is Dying is in memory of Lynn Edgar Semega.

Acknowledgments

Thank you to the editors of the following journals, where some of these poems first appeared, sometimes in alternate versions:

Blast Furnace Press, "Sappho" & "Different Death"

Comstock Review, "Portrait of Mother on the Greek Peninsula" & "Oneiric Means Dreamlike"

First Literary Review East, "Apollo Rising" & "Walking Home from the Poetry Salon"

Gravel, "Nike Adjusting Her Sandal" (pp. 25 & 32)

Haibun Today, "Eight Years After" (as "Epistle: Eight Years After") & "Eye of the Needle"

It's All About Arts, "Driving to Lake Erie on Mother's 97th Birthday"

Lily Poetry Review, "On Thira"

Literary Bohemian, "Thessaloniki, 4 AM" (as "Thessaloniki, Four A.M.")

Main Street Rag, "Self Portrait as Jane Kenyon"

Mason Street Review, "Ars Poetica" (p.8), "Bittersweet" & "Point of Origin"

masspoetry.org, "Tinos, August 2012" was "Poem of the Moment"

RHINO, "the modern poet tries to read Sappho in ancient Greek"

Right Hand Pointing, "The Day Jack Gilbert Kissed Me"

SWWIM, "I Will Forgive"

Thrush Poetry Journal, "Sappho in Translation"

Joe Gouveia Outermost Poetry Contest, Marge Piercy, Judge: "End of Life Directive" and "Self Portrait As Lot's Wife" were awarded honorable mention.

Best of the Net: "Ars Poetica" (p.8) was honored as a finalist.

To those who helped these poems, thank you: The Poetry Workshop at the Boston Center for Adult Education, led by Tom Daley. The Concord Poetry Center, and the Colrain Manuscript Conference: thank you Joan Houlihan for believing in these poems. The Wellfleet Poetry Workshop, my gratitude and love to Marge Piercy. Thank you to my poet friends and readers. There are too many to list here, but special thanks to Jenny Grassl, Lisa Kaufman, Eve Linn, Laura Billie Moss, Kyle Potvin, Sarah Dickinson Snyder, and Marjorie Thomsen.

My gratitude to my parents, Jerry and Katherine Vassos, who gave me the gift of two native languages; to my husband, Gary Koeppel, and to my sister Donna Vassos, for their support – I love you so much.

About the Author

Anastasia Vassos was born in Cleveland, OH. She earned her BA from Kalamazoo College and her MBA from the School of Management at Simmons College. She is an alumna of the Colrain Manuscript Conference and Breadloaf Writers Conference. A reader for *Lily Poetry Review*, she speaks three languages, and is a long-distance cyclist. She lives in Boston with her husband.

42° 19′ 47.9″ N 70° 56′ 43.9″ W

Nixes Mate is a navigational hazard in Boston Harbor used during the colonial period to gibbet and hang pirates and mutineers.

Nixes Mate Books features small-batch artisanal literature, created by writers who use all 26 letters of the alphabet and then some, honing their craft the time-honored way: one line at a time.

nixesmate.pub